Seeking Whispers

By

Peter D Hehir

PETER D. HEHIR

P. D Hehir

2022

First published in the United Kingdom in 2021 by
The Big Poetry Project

ISBN 979 - 8 - 48243 - 362 - 1

' I threw a stone of Innocence
Across the empty sea,
It landed on some other shore
As guilty as can be.'

Peter D Hehir
2021

Contents

Grey Hair is God's Graffiti

When youth gets lost in wrinkles
And your knees don't bend the same,
When all the world is passing go,
But you're further in the game.

With the lamplights slowly dimming,
As the darkness lost the bet,
There are pictures made of history,
With the moments you forget.

As your eyes can see the future,
Though we all can see the truth,
That there's fire in your belly still,
But there's snowflakes on the roof.

As the Autumn fast approaches
And the seasons take the blame,
When all the world is passing go,
But you're further in the game.

Where Starlings Fly

Blindfold me down, where the leaves are brown
And the trees just stand and wait,
Cover my ears, where the wind disappears
And the fire just burns in the grate.

Walk with me through, where the skies are blue
And the clouds kiss time goodbye,
Dance with me round, those puddles we found,
Where the last known starlings fly.

Sit with me where, the lost say a prayer
And the clouds just burst with white,
As the verses play, in the light of day
And the pens begin to write.

Blindfold me down, where the leaves are brown
And the trees just stand and wait,
As the daylight fades, in the great parades
And the sunset knows it fate.

Silent Shout

Rouge soft of battle hardened skin,
Let me in.
Dark breaking heart with silent shout,
Let me out.

Twisted soul of torment never free,
Let me be.
Cold aching soul I'm walking with,
Let me live.

Dying promise made to not believe,
Let me breathe.
Painful kiss of truth to never lie,
Let me die.

Crushing curse of wishes left to make,
Let me break.
Raging pulse too lonely to depend,
Let me mend.

Tangled web of worry left to weave,
Let me breathe.
Empty shadows falling to the sky,
Let me die.

Tired weary heart of loves decree,
Let me be.
Wild words to take but never give,
Let me live.

Breaking walls of worry paper thin,
Let me in.
Burning eyes in tears full of doubt,
Let me out.

Beyond the Pale

Through Flanders, Somme and Passchendaele,
We did not bend nor break or fail,
Where life came through beyond the pale,
Through Flanders, Somme and Passchendaele.

Those eyes of Ypres haunt us still,
Through open wounds and broken quill,
When trained to die but not to kill,
Those eyes of Ypres haunt us still.

Those sounds of Jutland shake the soul
Through horses eyes and dying foal,
When onward march the bell would toll,
Those sounds of Jutland shake the soul.

The spring offensive came too soon,
By sunlight stars or sheltered moon,
We died again that afternoon,
The spring offensive came too soon.

As Amiens would stir the blood
Of British boots on foreign mud,
And die once more we knew we would,
As Amiens would stir the blood.

Through Flanders, Somme and Passchendaele,
We did not bend nor break or fail,
Where life came through beyond the pale,
Through Flanders, Somme and Passchendaele.

.

Do Dogs Get Pins and Needles?

Do dogs get pins and needles?
Do cats get scared of heights?
Can bees come down with hay fever
Or moths get bored of lights?

Do crabs think we walk sideways?
Do lions think we roar?
Does an insect think it's finally free,
As it crawls beneath the door?

Do zebras think they're black or white?
Do penguins think the same?
Can a fish forget to swim sometimes?
Does a tiger think it's tame?

Do turtles think they're homeless?
Do wasps just think we dance?
Does a tortoise never leave the house
But to only eat the plants?

Do leopards think we're missing spots?
Or spiders think we're shy?
Do birds think that our arms are wings
But we've never tried to fly?

Do owls ever get eye strain?
Or ants just think we're tall?
There are things we'll never know about
These creatures great and small.

The Human Race

When the light turns into darkness,
Yet the world will still remain,
We have skin of different colours,
But our blood is just the same.

When you're treated like a shadow
And the colour fits the crime,
When all the world is watching,
Like you should be doing time.

As our history conditions us,
Our minds are black and white
But night can't live without the day,
Nor day without the night.

So when the race is over,
Each race will still remain,
We have skin of different colours,
But our blood is just the same.

Sonnet 21

How dare I step into the dying shade?
And ask questions of those who never lie,
I claim on my life that heaven's manmade,
As we all die a death that paupers die.
What keeps us going when we know the end?
Trapped in a solitude of twisted fate,
Light of day will on darkness depend,
If we live like peasants or kings; we wait.
How cruel a life that dreams are left undreamt?
But nightmares fill the tears that mourners weep
And devils hands and angels harps do tempt,
The weakest souls of those who want to sleep.
If death be simply the meaning of life,
To her I'll propose and call her my wife.

Waiting at the Lights

There's a song on the radio
But I don't know the words,
So I whistle them softly
Like the last of the birds

Then I tap on the wheel
To the summertime blues,
But I turn up the volume
For the start of the news.

And it's nothing but chaos,
Simply, death and despair,
As eyes turn to watching,
For a break light repair.

Now the engines are revving,
Just to exit the scene
And the world is just waiting
For the amber and green.

Nothing Changes

A snake can always shed its skin
But will always be a snake,
A river can be dry or deep
But will never be a lake.

A raindrop can be big or small
But will always come out wet,
A moment only happens once,
To remember or forget.

A spoken word will never die,
As it lives from when it's said,
A thought can never really live
If it's still inside your head.

A picture can be photoshopped
But the camera never lies,
A grave can hold a tramp or king
But will never change in size.

The earth it might be flat or round
But it's never ours to own,
A seed is all you need for life
But first it must be sewn.

The sun can never really fall
And the night can never break,
A snake can always shed its skin
But will always be a snake.

And They Wore Black

Carry me in at the start of the day,
Sing me a hymn in an old fashioned way,
A burden too heavy, too heavy to bare,
Wiping your eyes at the start of the prayer.

Where eulogies mix with a symphony sweet,
The story shall end that I didn't complete,
So rise in the pews with a bellowing verse,
Singing the news of the horse and the hearse.

Lament at the life, as the living lament,
Bow in the grief like the broken and bent,
Where the candles return but only to be,
A flame to be forged in the passing of me.

So dust off your knees and walk to the song
Of something inside, inside me so strong,
Then on with your lives if only to say;
Carry me out at the end of the day.

Running with Scissors

Chaos controls me,
Folds and unrolls me,
Taking me right to the edge.
Chaos pursues me,
Tries to confuse me,
Standing up high on a ledge.

Fear attacks me,
Hits 'til it cracks me,
Shattering all that it stole.
Fear defines me,
Hunts and unwinds me,
Splintering through to my soul.

Wisdom betrays me,
Swings and it sways me,
Lost in a mind full of sin.
Wisdom berates me,
Makes out it hates me,
Stops all the light coming in.

Beauty belies me,
Fits 'til it tries me,
Dying in wars that it won.
Beauty deceives me,
Walks out and leaves me,
Not looking back 'til it's done.

Vera Lynn

Those white cliffs are mourning
Where the bluebirds have flown,
As the dark clouds are breaking,
Now you're heading on home.

We are waving goodbye now,
So, please say hello
To the loved ones we've lost
And the people we know.

When the rainclouds come over
Or a new day appears,
In the love and the laughter,
The war and the tears.

Go sing like a sweetheart,
Where the sunshine will be,
And we'll meet you again
Where the bluebirds are free.

Cupid's Claws

I saw you turn the lights off
So I couldn't find the door,
Then I stepped on all those Lego bricks
Left strewn across the floor

I tiptoed through the darkness
Where shadows met the night,
With wounds I never had before
Just searching for the light.

As all the walls were listening
To feelings in decline,
You knew that I was yours to keep
But not that you were mine.

The floor became so slippery
With carpets full of lies,
For love was just a game you played
And hate was just the prize.

My body fell to tiredness,
The night had come and gone,
I stretched with hope and bitterness
To turn the lights back on.

But when I found the light switch
I had seen too many wars,
You had left me torn apart again,
By Cupid and his claws.

Forever Young

There's a poppy in the chorus
Of the song you never sung,
For the autumn never saw us,
May you stay forever young.

There's a helmet in the soil
Where the battle came to be,
As the scene will start to spoil,
With the burden of the free.

There's a tunnel in the trenches
That aches with every beat,
With names on all the benches
That never knew defeat.

But you shall live forever
On the tip of every tongue,
And we'll always be together,
May you stay forever young.

Eyes Full of Tiers

My skin is drunk on alcohol
From Anti Bac and wipes,
Where hidden smiles suffocate
In masks of many types.

There's tiers in our eyes again
From posters on the walls,
That tell us what we shouldn't do
Until the number falls.

With condensated shield screens
I stumble through the streets,
But buses, trains and aeroplanes
Are full of empty seats.

As rollercoaster graphs are shown
To scare us half to death,
For every time we tried to breathe
We couldn't catch our breath.

There's sale signs in the all shops,
While some are closing down,
We are living by percentages
Within this crazy town.

There's rainbows stuck in window panes
With multicoloured stripes,
But my skin is drunk on Alcohol
From Anti Bac and wipes.

What Nonsense is Time?

What nonsense is time,
When the morrow comes all too soon?
Where the shadows of life doth climb,
And the rosebud is tempted to bloom.

What nonsense is time,
When all but the dying is done?
And the stars in the sky realign,
As the moon sees the last of the sun.

What nonsense is time,
When light loses light of its own?
Oh the bells of the living do chime,
In the sweetest goodbye they have known.

What nonsense is time,
When the sun sees the last of the moon?
Where the shadows of life doth climb,
And the rosebud is tempted to bloom.

The Mourning of the Crows

There's a blemish in the bloodline
Of our history they say,
There's a fault in every landmine
That we step on every day.

There's a shark inside the water
We have tested with our toes,
Like a lamb led to the slaughter,
At the mourning of the crows.

There's a world outside the window
And the lyrics made you look,
There's a story on the slideshow,
But you've never read the book.

For we heard it on the grapevine
We are actors in a play,
There's a blemish in the bloodline
And we're bleeding every day.

The Lonely Hours

I've dreamt through flowers
And lived through thorns,
I've sat for hours
In the thunderstorms.

I've loved through fears
And lost through pain,
I've counted tears
In the pouring rain.

I've danced on frost
And walked on snow,
I've seen them lost
In the fire below.

I've flown with birds
And crashed with ease,
I've whispered words
To the tallest trees.

I've climbed on clouds
And fell from stars,
I've seen those shrouds
Hide a million scars.

I've lived through thorns
And dreamt through flowers,
I've watched those storms
In the lonely hours.

Broken Telephone

Blow me down with feathers, blow me down,
There's rumours flying round this crazy town,
There's a pauper in the doorway with a crown,
So blow me down with feathers, blow me down.

Seek me out in fiction, seek me out,
There's whispers that we need to talk about,
There's secrets in the stories that we shout,
Seek me out in fiction, seek me out.

Wish me well when leaving, wish me well,
There's a little piece of heaven in the hell,
There's lies that only curtain twitchers tell,
Wish me well when leaving, wish me well.

Blow me down with feathers, blow me down,
There's a tumour in the stomach of the town,
The king is in his palace with a frown,
Blow me down with feathers, blow me down.

One Last Breath

When death pulls out its sharpest sword
And puts life on a chopping board,
To take a breath and cut the cord,
I'll be there at the end.

When death pulls out its poisoned tongue,
To mock the climb of every rung,
I'll take your soul from mouth to lung,
On me you can depend.

When death pulls out it gun to shoot
And laces up its battered boot,
I'll silence it by pressing mute,
And in the troops I'll send.

When death pulls out its rope to hang
The very words that life had sang,
Upon that drum I'll gently bang
Your name until the end.

The Loudest Quiet

The loudest quiet ever
Was the heartbreak that occurred,
When we reached a place called never,
Where nothing could be heard.

The longest shortest silence
Was the gap we never filled,
In a splintered soul of violence,
Where the doubt was never killed

The greatest disappointment
Was the future that we met,
Like a bite without the ointment,
In a bittersweet regret.

The loudest quiet ever
Was the heartbreak that occurred,
When I broke in two forever
And you didn't say a word.

Going to the Dentist

Your mouth looks like a graveyard
But no one's coming in,
In the brightest room of drilling doom
Where the painful times begin

So now the chair is lowering,
And the light is in your eyes,
As you hear a voice say open wide,
Now your pulse is on the rise.

Then pausing, prodding, poking
As they count along the curve,
There are implements and Instruments
That will get on every nerve.

And the fillings in those sandwiches
Will be haunting you today,
When you're swapping them for other ones
As your tongue gets in the way.

But they must be playing battleships,
With the codes they start to shout
And the words ring like an epitaph;
"We'll have to pull it out!"

A Place for the Winter

My souls still got scars from the summer,
From the nights that I slept in the park,
Now my hearts found a place for the winter
But I still go to sleep in the dark.

My curtains are open to moonlight
So I don't have to sleep in that dark,
And my eyes have a battle with midnight
From the nights that I slept in the park.

The stars in the sky were a cover,
From the nights that I slept in the park,
And I know I won't find me another,
Because I still go to sleep in the dark

Now my cigarettes burning like fire,
So I don't have to sleep in the dark,
And the bells they still ring from the spire,
Through the nights that I spent in the park.

Mr. Bumble

I'm off to go and pollinate
Which flower shall I choose?
As I sit on this banana skin
Before it gets a bruise.

I'll whizz on past the apples trees
And down into the grass,
Where summer drinks are covered up
With cling film on the glass.

To stop me diving into them
And spoiling all the fun,
When people see me flying there
They just get up and run.

But I'm just there to pollinate
Before the light will lose,
I'll ask again before I go
Which flower shall I choose?

Great Scott!

Someone clamped my time machine
Way back in '84,
I had to live my life again
But different from before.

I left myself a note or two
Of all the things to see,
And tried to help myself become
The man I want to be.

I saw the clowns of history
That made me go astray,
And witnessed way too many sins,
Then looked the other way.

But all the fun will start again,
The days have come and gone,
For I've unclamped my time machine,
In Twenty Twenty One.

Fire and Sand

Sit with me now
If time will allow,
Let's look at the stars
Of the bear and the plough.

Draw on my hand
Just as we planned,
With fingertips full
Of fire and sand.

Cancel the war
Just like before,
That lead me to love
In the circle and soar.

Hold me so tight
By the darkness and light,
And lets fight the moon
For the best of the night.

Swings and Roundabouts

It's all just swings and roundabouts
When there's just no place to hide,
There's courage on the monkey bars
And a tantrum on the slide.

The seesaws got a strop on,
And the tunneled tubes are broke,
The tyres all look deflated now,
Is this some kind of joke?

The sandpits got a warning sign
That is close to blowing down,
There's benches full of crying kids,
With an ice cream covered frown.

And now it's raining cats and dogs
So we'll have to go inside,
It's all just swings and roundabouts,
When there's just no place to hide.

Lend me your Wings

Lend me your wings,
For I won't fly far,
To where it begins,
On the edge of a scar.

I'll set off at sunrise,
When the wind is awake,
The birdsong will guide me,
On the route that I take.

I wish to see freedom
And the joy that it brings,
With the biggest of smiles,
From the smallest of things.

So I bid you goodnight,
For the time is a foe,
To a pillow that's calling,
Where the other ones go.

Now the morning is here,
As I take to the air,
Through the wonderful colours
And the clouds that they wear.

But the day paints a picture,
That the darkness forgets,
Of a land slowly dying,
Like the sun as it sets.

But I see fear living
With the brave and the good,
Next to rivers of plastic
Getting lost in the flood.

I've seen all the sadness
The hope and the pain,
The world wasn't healing,
So I flew back again

Now here are your wings
For I didn't fly far,
To see all the battles,
On the edge of a scar.

Heartbreak Overload

I'm peeling my soul off the ceiling,
I'm scrapping my heart off the wall,
My body is broken and healing,
Where the shadows are skinny and tall.

I'm sinking like stones in a river,
I'm rising like floods in storm,
My mind is alight with shiver,
Where once it was cosy and warm.

I'm starving like wolves in the wild,
I'm aching like never before,
My life is so suddenly mild,
Where once it was hot to the core.

I'm taking to kneeling and praying,
I'm hoping you threw what I caught,
Those kisses are slowly decaying,
Where the shadows and stubby and short.

When

When a moment becomes a memory
And a wish becomes a prayer,
I went to sit and rest a while
But you kicked away the chair.

When a scene becomes a photograph,
And a gift becomes a curse,
When a Poet runs out of ink again
At the start of the following verse.

When a

31

Envy

You said I walked on water
Because I knew I couldn't swim,
In a dark green pool of jealousy
That you filled up to the brim.

For your soul was made in China
Like the whispers that you told,
But the truth is still in nappies,
As the lies are getting old.

Your lips tend to exaggerate
And so on the story goes,
I just bumped into Pinocchio
And he's asking for his nose.

Now the green eyed monster's crying
And the outlooks rather grim,
For you said I walked on water
Because I knew I couldn't swim.

Broken Thoughts

I'm cursed with tired eyes
Like a plague of butterflies,
In their beautiful disguise,
As I'm cursed with tired eyes.

I'm cursed with broken thought,
In as mind so out of sorts,
Lost love on tennis courts,
I'm cursed with broken thoughts.

I'm cursed with untouched time,
With such beauty in the crime
Of a verse that didn't rhyme,
I'm cursed with untouched time.

I'm cursed with tired eyes
And a smile full of lies,
But I'll try it on for size,
When I'm cursed with tired eyes.

Nan and Grandad's

There's candles on the mantelpiece
And warmth in the all the chairs,
There's grandad in that winter fleece
The snowman never wears.

As grandma sets the coal alight
Where lines are gently cast,
By the Tiger! Tiger! burning bright
And the poems of the past.

That float across each battered beam
And roll across the walls,
As softly as a child's dream
Or a snowflake as it falls.

With soda bread for suppertime
And smiles for dessert,
As grandma pours a glass of wine
With flour on her skirt.

Now grandads in his dressing gown
With slippers made to match,
As winter lays it's blanket down
Upon our knitted thatch.

And I'm sitting in the rocking chair
In the hope of growing old,
To be like Nan and Grandad there,
With stories to be told.

Music

With passers-by performing to designer earphones,
I lip read all their lyrics, from Sinatra to the Stones.
They use a fresh air drum kit and a symbol in their shoe,
As they pluck a fake guitar string to the Beatles or The Who.
Then they smile at the chorus, like they wrote those very words,
Just whistling out a melody, from Oasis to the Birds.
Those Whitney Houston wanderers come belting out a tune,
As ground control is listening to the man inside the moon.
They stroll on like the Bee Gees as they try to stay alive,
They waltz across the paving slabs then break into a jive.
As they tap their toes so knowingly when Elton's lyrics flow,
Then WHAM! it wakes them up again before they have to go.
They play on with their fingertips to Queen and Billy Joel
And bring to life within their hips the King of Rock and Roll.
Then an Artist fills their headphones and they smile to the sky,
As Purple Rain comes pouring down and doves begin to cry.
But the day begins to fade-away as the stars begin to show
And they pause there playlist for the night when Lionel says 'Hello'.
Then they stumble up their stairways to the night's forgotten beats,
Now there's music in my bedroom and a tune beneath the sheets.

Smokescreens

Tomato sauce and stuntmen
And Gunfire on record,
Wounds that wipe off easily
From a papier-mâché sword.

Whiskey made of apple juice
And beer just the same,
There's credits not an epitaph
For every person's name.

Trenches made of furniture,
Snow from old machines,
The only real shots are from
The camera to our screens.

With Scenery that folds away
And limbs that never break,
Where life has got a second chance
To do a second take.

Together We Stand

There's a bottle of hindsight
That I keep in the fridge,
Like a boat of regret
Under yesterday's bridge.

We won't be defeated
With hearts being strong,
There is peace in our lyrics
And there's love in our song.

So walk with me now
Through the battles ahead,
Like an army of giants,
Until the terror is dead.

And I'll carry you on
Like the weight of a feather,
For together we'll stand,
As we're standing together.

The Grey Area

If you broke a birds wings
But then told it to fly?
If you gave me your heart
And then left me to die?
I would give you the truth
But then tell you a lie,

For you was right,
But so was I.

If I scribbled my name
On the picture you drew?
If I doubted your eyes
For a moment or two?
You would tell me the words
That I already knew,

For I was wrong,
But so were you.

If you told me a joke
But then told me cry?
If you questioned my words
With a 'where'? and a 'why'?
I would hang up our hopes
For a dreamer to buy,

For you was right,
But so was I

If I told you to guess
But then gave you a clue?
If I showed you the sky
But had painted it blue?
You would give me your heart
And tell me it's new,

For I was wrong,
But so were you.

Wednesday

It snowed on Wednesday Morning
Just like the story said,
And the sunrise gave a warning,
As I stumbled out of bed.

My clothes cluttered the bedroom floor
And my coffee cup was cold,
The droplets that the morning saw,
They were only minutes old.

The snowmen in the empty street
We're made to melt away,
My slippers hugged my tired feet,
At the breaking of the day.

So I gave into the yawning
And I climbed back into bed,
For it snowed on Wednesday morning,
Just like the story said.

I Left the Tap Running

I left the tap running
Just to drown out the noise,
Of the wild ones coming,
With their battleship toys.

I left the tap running
Just to drown out the sound,
Of the hummingbird humming,
When there's no one around.

I left the tap running
Just to drown out the play
Of the thumbs that were strumming,
In the heat of the day.

I left the tap running
Just to drown out the noise,
Of the wild ones coming,
With their battleship toys.

To Love

This is to you love,
The way you care and kiss
And reminisce.
This is to you love,
The way you sing and dance
In wild romance.
This is to you love,
The way to bend and break
And give and take.
This is to you love,
The way you laugh and cry
And wonder why.
This is to you love,
The way you fall and fade
With memories made.
This is to you love,
The way you lie and tease,
And die with ease.
This is to you love,
The way you make and mend
Until the end.
This is to you love,
The way you burst and bloom
And leave the room.
This is to you love,
The way you splinter through
The black and blue.

This is to you love,
This is to you.

Batteries Not Included

My brain just had a hiccup
Now nothing seems to work,
There's cages full of question marks
That tried to go berserk.

I'm anchored in my thinking
To every wild thought,
When dragged across the promenade
But never to be caught.

There's vessels in the harbour,
That never tried to float,
I went to change the channel once
But lost the new remote.

My mind is at the menders
Now it's nearly 10 to 1
And It broke up like a jigsaw,
When I tried to turn it on.

Hold Hands, Not Grudges

'So where are you from?' The blind man said,
"I'm from a place where the world is dead."
'It can't be true' he then replied,
'I closed my eyes, I never died.'

'So where are you going?' The deaf man signed,
"Off to a place to help the blind."
'I'm coming to!' He said with glee,
'To hear the sound of being free.'

'Can I come too?' The dumb man wrote,
'I'll watch the waves and steer the boat'
But I said, "No I'll walk alone,
Until hearts are full and minds have grown."

They looked upset but understood,
That if they came the others would,
So I turned to them and simply said;
"You are alive, but the world is dead."

The Drunken Wasp

Like a drunken wasp on a window sill,
Having spent last night in the daffodil,
Yes that was such a bitter pill to take.
I was smiling when the sun went down,
As the night put on its dressing gown,
Oh the times I wish that I had stayed awake.

I've slept and stirred in the beds of flowers,
Got lost sometimes in April showers
And went to swim the tide before it came.
Then watched the seasons start to shout,
Though all the cracks within the drought,
As certain parts of nature took the blame.

In the throes of time where dreams are free
And the petals blow with history,
I'm basking like a shadow in the sun.
When all that came and all I saw
Was nectar from the night before
And spiderwebs of silk still being spun.

So I'm kicking leaves up off the grass
Just waiting for the time to pass,
With photographs my eyes forgot to take.
There's happiness within in the stars
Like a million burning old cigars,
And constellations keeping me awake.

Uninstalled Anxiety

I've uninstalled anxiety,
Deleted pain and fear,
I've memorised the manual,
Then made it disappear.

I've saved up all the happy times
And wiped the system clean,
I've transferred all my worries out
To someone else's screen.

I've blocked out all the viruses
That made me go insane,
I've filtered out the bad results
Then tried to search again.

I've pulled the plug on loneliness
It's not allowed in here,
I've memorised the manual
And made it disappear.

The Hero

My next kiss will tell you
What's left to be said,
But you look in my eyes
For a picture instead.

My next kiss completes you
Like trees full of birds,
But my smile defeats you
In wars without words

My next kiss will hurt you
Like nothing before,
But my verses will sooth you
Like words without war.

My next kiss will tell you
What's left to be said,
But the story is told
And the hero is dead.

Funeral Rain

It soaked me to the bone it did,
As I mourned the very sun,
My shirt was get smaller still,
As the buttons came undone.

My shoes were once the cleanest pair,
They were blacker than the hearse,
As I tripped up on a paving slab
And only made them worse.

With my expectations lowering
Above and in the grave,
The mourners stood on either side,
Where rain clouds misbehave.

So we waddled like a colony,
Of those penguins in the mud,
It soaked me to the bone it did,
The only way it could.

Splendid Isolation

The people lived in houses
And did what they were told,
With siblings, friends and spouses,
The young ones and the old.

They tended to their gardens
And sunbathed in the nude
With 'what's' and 'beg your pardons',
Depending on their mood.

They gathered their opinions
And sent them on their way,
But ran back in like minions
When their leader came to play.

They flicked through all the channels
But all they ever saw,
Where quiz show bloody panels,
Just like the day before.

They clicked on apps to order
And paid a costly sum,
But hunger crossed the border,
By the time that it had come.

Then in splendid isolation
The young became the old,
And the old became the nation,
Just doing what they're told.

The World is on Snooze

We've hit the snooze button
And gone back to bed,
With a hope for tomorrow
Where it's safer instead.

We lay back and ponder
That North South Divide,
Who thought there'd be tiers,
Once the tears had tried.

Like the signs in the window
Are the signs of the times,
So we're keeping our distance
When we're waiting in lines.

As adverts for safety
Pop up on our screens,
But we've seen it before
And we know what it means.

Just caught in our bubbles
And told not to mix,
In homes or in gardens
Or a party of six.

We check for the latest
As we lay there and wonder,
If the figures they tell us
Will be over or under.

But the cases are rising
As the hopes going down,
There's a band called restriction
And they're playing in town.

Now the world is still drowning
In yesterday's news,
So when the alarm goes
Just put it on snooze.

Light of Hope

Beneath the mask there lies a face
Where battle lines are drawn,
To find the light of hope that shines,
Through every broken dawn.

No capes or titles needed here
Or medals to be shown,
These soldiers fight another war,
In a world they've never known.

But unrelenting on they fight,
With death upon their heels,
In crowded wars and corridors,
Where a worn out angel kneels.

So when you rest your head to sleep,
There are heroes being born,
Who find the light of hope that shines,
Through every broken dawn.

Salt and Sugar

Salt and Sugar look the same,
Be careful who you trust,
For You and I both have a name
But we shall turn to dust.

As shadows need the very sun
That caused them all to die,
We only ever load the gun
To watch the bullets fly.

A diamond is a lump of coal
That made it out alive,
A ghost is just a tired soul
That wanted to survive.

A seed is just a future plant
That hasn't seen the light,
An Ant is just a flying Ant
That didn't make the flight.

A star is just a dying rock
But still we see it shine,
A man could be a laughing stock
Then read the second line.

Now losers have to play the game
But winning is a must,
For Salt and Sugar look the same,
Be careful who you trust.

Bruises

I cut myself shaving
When they knocked on the door,
To ask me what happened,
In the evening before.

It stung like an insult
Or a prick from a thorn,
And it started on bleeding
Where the tissue was torn.

I wiped down the mirror
And turned off the taps,
My mind was a compass
Upon yesterday's maps.

I searched for the feeling
And hoped for a spark,
To help me remember
Going home in the dark.

I looked through the spy-hole
At trouble and fate,
As karma was lifting
The latch on the gate.

But I couldn't remember
As I opened the door,
I was covered in bruises
From the evening before.

The Primark Pilgrims

The pilgrims of Primark
And the gannets of Greggs,
Camp on the pavements
In a tent without pegs.

They cuddle their Costa's
In the wild outdoors,
Then sail through aisles
For the sales in stores.

With an empty old Burtons
And those derelicts shops,
Where the Amazon's flowing
But life never stops.

They all come to worship,
For the kicks and the thrills,
They pray for a bargain
And they pay at that tills.

The queues keep on growing
So it's my cue to leave,
Through the crowds and the traffic,
Where I wonder and weave.

To sit on my sofa,
With the weights off my legs,
And the world rushing past me,
Like a tent without pegs.

I'll Think of You

Every time a lily falls
And every time a sparrow calls,
In shooting stars like cannonballs,
I'll think of you.

Every time the thunder breaks
And every time the wind awakes,
On river banks and frozen lakes,
I'll think of you.

Every time the ending nears
And every time the frost appears,
On garden grass like souvenirs,
I'll think of you.

Every time an eagle soars
And every time a tiger roars,
In treetops high and forest floors,
I'll think of you.

A Better Place

My heart feels like a trampoline
That's found a better place,
Where sadness does a somersault
And falls flat on its face.

The springs all play a symphony
Where earth and science meet,
As laughter does a pirouette
And lands back on its feet.

With music lying motionless
So love can just prepare,
When sound performs a ballet dance
With silence in the air.

So lay your violins to rest
When pulses set the pace,
My heart feels like a trampoline
That's found a better place.

Finally Home

Draw all the curtains, dim all the lights,
Turn all the 'No's' into maybes and might's,
Flick on the kettle, turn on the taps,
Sit by the fire for a moment perhaps.
Cuddle your coffee, curl up your toes,
Smell the aroma where the bubble bath goes.
Step out your slippers, slip out your robe,
Rest in the bath like you've travelled the globe.
Wallow in water, wrinkle in peace,
Empty your thoughts in a restless release.
Blow out the candies, pull out the plug,
Cling to the towel as it gives you a hug.
Shake to a shiver as cold as the brew
That you left by the fire for a moment or two.
Sink in the sofa, when eyelids collapse,
Walk into dreamland for a moment perhaps.
Rise like a zombie, reset the pose,
Turn all the maybes into 'Nevers' and 'No's'.
Circle the kitchen, out come the swears
Stubbing your toes and the table and chairs.
Block out the throbbing, lock all the doors,
Yawn like those hippos with double set jaws.
Wake from the slumber, head off to bed,
Climb up the stairs like a dreamer instead.
Shut out the sirens, turn off the phone,
Fluff up your pillows, you're finally home.

A Cure for Sorrow

There's a cure for sorrow, it's you.
There's a pill for the darkness, it's blue.

There's a hope for the flowers, it's rain.
There's a doubt in the shadows, it's pain.

There's a close to the doubting, it's proof.
There's a battle for justice, it's truth.

There's a sound to the season, it's song.
There's a curse for the righteous, it's wrong.

There's a game for the hunter, it's prey.
There's a mould for the maker, it's clay.

There's an edge to the climax, it's near.
There's a risk in the gamble, it's fear.

There's an end to the whisper, it's loud.
There's a reason for nature, it's proud.

There's a path for the child, it's laid.
There's a debt for the soldier, it's paid.

There's a meaning to darkness, it's light.
There's a cloud in the water, it's white.

There's a partner for trouble, it's strife.
There's a wish for the wild, it's life.

There's a song for the magpie, it's true.
There's a cure for sorrow, it's two.

Behind the Mask

I smiled at a stranger
But no one saw a thing,
The only common part of us
Was hanging by a string.

The rain it started falling
But mine was waterproof,
My steamed up pair of glasses
We're blocking out the truth.

My phone it started ringing
In a pocket full of soap,
Surrounded by bacteria
That washed away the hope.

I pressed the green to answer
And held it to my face,
The caller searched my muffled words
To track and then to trace.

They simply couldn't hear me,
I had to end the call
As I went my sip my coffee cup
I ended up the fool.

So I think you should be thankful
That you cannot hear me sing,
Beneath my facial underwear
Just hanging by a string.

Betelgeuse

You tried Orion's Belt on
But it didn't seem to fit,
I took an arrow from the sky
And put some holes in it.

As red became your future,
Your present and your past,
A being made so beautiful
But never made to last.

A champagne kind of whirlwind
Like diamonds in the sky,
To live a million years or more,
Then curl on up to die.

As the super giants gathered
Where the supernovas split,
I took the constellation down
And put some holes in it.

The Right Side of the Grass

Just whistle while you walk along,
Give thanks to all you pass
And know that you're just living life
The right side of the grass.

Be kind in everything you do
And everything you say,
For tomorrow might depend on all
The things you do today.

Give voice to all the quiet ones
Who simply can't be heard,
Let actions be your guiding light
And peace be in your word.

You'll never get a second chance
To see the things you pass,
So know that your just living life
The right side of the grass.

The Strength and Stay
(In Memory of Prince Phillip)

From the island of Greece,
To a man of the crown,
We pay our respects,
With the lights going down.

On a royal so regal,
With a humorous tongue,
So proud like a soldier
In the song that he sung.

Like an anthem for living,
That won't go away,
As he quickly became
The strength and the stay.

A consort of courage,
To serve with a pride
Like a rock of the country
With his Queen by his side.

A prince of the people
With the strength of a king,
And forever revered,
In the song that we sing.

Now flags start to lower
In each city and town,
We will pay our respects
With the lights going down.

Dear Mother Nature

Dear Mother Nature
It's a while since we spoke,
How have you been getting on
In the litter and the smoke?

I heard that you were dying
And that times were rather bad,
It stirred up all the memories
Of the better times we had.

When the sun was always shining
And the joy would never end,
You'd turn on all the evening stars
For the messages I'd send.

Then I'd wake up in the morning
With a smile so big and wide,
For when I drew the curtains back
I would see that you've replied.

But now I'm reminiscing
Of a time that's come and gone,
I'm hoping you can find the strength
To turn the lights back on.

For I know you are a fighter
And I wish I could be there,
To teach the people how to live
And love and laugh and care.

But I know that you can show them,
If they only want to learn,
Their journey on this world will stop
If you didn't make it turn.

So I'll end my letter here,
And I pray that you will cope,
Until the day we meet again
I am yours forever - Hope.